SOMEWHERE TO TURN

Perspectives on Gifted and Talented Education

SOMEWHERE TO TURN
Strategies for Parents of Gifted and Talented Children

Eleanor G. Hall
Specialist Gifted and Talented
University of Wisconsin-Green Bay

Nancy Skinner
President
Michigan Association for the Academically Talented

Perspectives on Gifted and Talented Education

Abraham J. Tannenbaum
Director

Elizabeth Neuman
Editor

Gifted and Talented Project
Teachers College, Columbia University

Teachers College, Columbia University
New York and London   1980

This work was developed under a contract with the U.S. Office of
Education, Department of Health, Education, and Welfare. However, the
content does not necessarily reflect the position or policy of that Agency,
and no official endorsement of these materials should be inferred.

Library of Congress Cataloging in Publication Data

Hall, Eleanor G
    Somewhere to turn.

    (Perspectives on gifted and talented education)
    Bibliography: p.
    Includes index.
    1. Gifted children—Education.   2. Talented
students.   3. Home and school.   I. Skinner, Nancy,
joint author.   II. Title.   III. Series.
LC3993.H33   371.95   80-14958
ISBN 0-8077-2589-7

Design by Romeo Enriquez

8   7   6   5   4   3   2   1
80   81   82   83   84   85   86   87
Printed in the U.S.A.

CONTENTS

TABLES

FIGURES

FOREWORD

Gifted children who draw attention to themselves—and not all do—through their precocity are constantly in the public eye, sometimes as stars, sometimes as sties. They cannot be ignored, but they can be neglected. Professionals and laymen alike have often reacted ambivalently to these children, appreciating their special qualities while doubting their right to special educational enrichment on the grounds that it smacks of elitism. There are educators who believe that the gifted can make it on their own without extra help and regard differentiated programs for such children as luxuries that are welcome when they are affordable and quickly disposable when they are not. What counts most according to this point of view is the "golden mean," or normalcy, as reflected in the normal curve of ability and performance. Whoever fails to measure up to the golden mean has a right to every kind of compensatory assistance; whoever exceeds levels of functioning that are normal or average for most children may receive applause but no extra attention. Rarely is thought given to the possibility that democratic education means stretching each child's mind to its own outer limits without injury to mental or physical health.

Fortunately growing interest in the gifted at school is helping sharpen public concern for the individualities of *all* children. Differentiated education is beginning to replace procrustean education, and fewer people are making a fetish of averageness in the normal curve. Yet, this new awareness that "sameness" and "equality" are *not* synonymous terms when they refer to educational opportunity has not always led to a clear understanding of existing knowledge in the field. A great many myths have masqueraded as truisms, and they tend to be reinforced rather than exploded in some of the awareness rallies, lectures, and workshops on behalf of gifted children. Even the professional literature has been affected by unsubstantiated claims about the nature and nurture of giftedness and by rhetoric that appeals more to the emotions than to reason.

It is time that some clearer impressions were recorded about the "state of the art" in understanding and educating the gifted in order to counterbalance some of the distortions, wishful thinking, overblown claims, and misdirected evangelism that has plagued the field. The intention of this Teachers College series of original monographs is to contribute to that kind of corrective. It has grown out of a federally supported contract to develop information products on key topics pertaining to the gifted and to bring them to the attention of the general public, including laymen and professionals. The authors have devoted considerable care to the content of their statements and the consequent impact on readers. Each writer is eminently qualified to make a balanced, meaningful contribution that avoids simply paraphrasing what others have said earlier. The aim is to inform through cogent presentations that can be appreciated by the widest possible audience ranging from those who want to be initiated to those who seek new insights into the field of educating the gifted.

Abraham J. Tannenbaum
Teachers College, Columbia University

INTRODUCTION

O<small>F ANY GROUP</small> that plays a role in the lives of children, parents are the least prepared. For most people, parenting is a process of trial and error. A look at the number of best-selling books on how to raise children attests to the desire of many to understand the nurturing process and how to foster their children's development. Parents of an exceptional child are usually far less prepared for this role and in even greater need of help, advice, and counseling (Ellis, 1977).

Schools, however, despite their concern for other categories of exceptionality, are not likely to provide much help or advice to parents of the gifted. As Dorothy Sisk (n.d.) has noted, little guidance or support is even given to the parents of gifted youngsters who are enrolled in special programs for the gifted, although few educators fail to list the importance of the home and school working together as agents of socialization and identity formation. Perhaps no other group of parents has been so maligned by educators, misunderstood by the general public, and generally relegated to the status of "pushy parents" (Ellis, 1977).

This book has been designed to give such parents "somewhere to turn" for guidance and for a better understanding of the gifted. It is also designed for parents who suspect their children might be gifted, but don't know how to determine it.

1

HOW TO DETERMINE IF YOUR CHILD IS GIFTED

I<small>T IS OBVIOUS</small> from parent interviews and research in the field that the gifted child defies being pigeonholed into any classification that may be constructed. Many of these children do exhibit their abilities early, and early identification is very important. It increases the likelihood that their emotional and educational needs will be met once they are discovered. Others, however, do not show their abilities until the middle elementary grades or later, so the identification process must be continuous.

Without proper identification, programing, and support, gifted children may begin regressing, hiding their abilities and developing personality changes by kindergarten. Yet it is not surprising that many parents are unable to determine advanced development, for they often do not know the rate at which average children develop and have no basis for comparison. They need some indication of "normal" development rates if they are to be better predictors of giftedness. Normal development rates, however, are but averages and subject to wide variation. Parents who take them too literally, or believe signs of giftedness must appear in all areas, have mistakenly been led to conclude that their child isn't gifted because of slowness in one or more areas. The areas, as one survey (Frinier, 1978) of mistaken parents showed, can be talking late (an individual who began talking at age three and earned a Ph.D in physics at age 22), walking late (alone at 20 months), late toilet training (said to be a common area), no interest in books or in learning to read until taught in first grade, and no interest in school work. Some of the parents were quite surprised to learn that their child was gifted. Having one child identified as gifted often helps parents to pick up such traits in their other children, but it has also led them to believe gifted siblings were average just because they were not as highly gifted.

Thus narrative descriptions of some of the characteristics of the gifted and parental comment and elaboration, along with developmental rates, are provided to give parents of possibly gifted children more information upon which to form an opinion.

1

AT PRESCHOOL AGE

The following development guidelines, Table 1, for normal average children were compiled from a variety of developmental timetables, including the Bayley Scales of Infant Development, the Gesell Developmental Schedules, and the Slosson Intelligence Test. Your child need not be advanced in all areas to be considered gifted. However, if your child is about 30 percent more advanced than average on most items in at least one section of the table—in general motor ability, fine motor ability, or cognitive language—there is reason to believe that he or she may be gifted or talented. For example, if an average child sits up alone at seven months, a child 30 percent more advanced would do so 2.10 months earlier (7 mos. x .30 = 2.10 mos.) or at 4.9 months of age (7 mos. - 2.1 mos. = 4.9 mos.).

TABLE 1: DEVELOPMENTAL GUIDELINES

General Motor Ability

	Normal Months	30% More Advanced
Lifts chin up when lying stomach down	1	0.7
Holds up both head and chest	2	1.4
Rolls over	3	2.1
Sits up with support	4	2.8
Sits alone	7	4.9
Stands with help	8	5.6
Stands holding on	9	6.3
Creeps	11	7.7
Stands alone well	11	7.7
Walks alone	12.5	8.75
Walks, creeping is discarded	15	10.5
Creeps up stairs	15	10.5
Walks up stairs	18	12.6
Seats self in chair	18	12.6
Turns pages of book	18	12.6
Walks down stairs one hand held	21	14.7
Walks up stairs holds rail	21	14.7
Runs well, no falling	24	16.8
Walks up and down stairs alone	24	16.8
Walks on tiptoe	30	21.0
Jumps with both feet	30	21.0
Alternates feet when walking up stairs	36	25.2

General Motor Ability (*continued*)

	Normal Months	30% More Advanced
Jumps from bottom step	36	25.2
Rides tricycle using pedals	36	25.2
Skips on one foot only	48	33.6
Throws ball	48	33.6
Skips alternating feet	60	42.0

Fine Motor Ability

	Normal Months	30% More Advanced
Grasps handle of spoon but lets go quickly	1	0.7
Vertical eye coordination	1	0.7
Plays with rattle	3	2.1
Manipulates a ball, is interested in detail	6	4.2
Pulls string adaptively	7	4.9
Shows hand preference	8	5.6
Holds object between fingers and thumb	9	6.3
Holds crayon adaptively	11	7.7
Pushes car alone	11	7.7
Scribbles spontaneously	13	9.1
Drawing imitates stroke	15	10.5
Folds paper once imitatively	21	14.7
Drawing imitates V stroke and circular stroke	24	16.8
Imitates V and H strokes	30	21.0
Imitates bridge with blocks	36	25.2
Draws person with two parts	48	33.6
Draws unmistakable person with body	60	42.0
Copies triangle	60	42.0
Draws person with neck, hands, clothes	72	50.4

Cognitive Language

	Normal Months	30% More Advanced
Social smile at people	1.5	1.05
Vocalizes four times or more	1.6	1.12

Cognitive Language *(continued)*

	Normal Months	30% More Advanced
Visually recognizes mother	2	1.4
Searches with eyes for sound	2.2	1.54
Vocalizes two different sounds	2.3	1.61
Vocalizes four different syllables	7	4.9
Says "da-da" or equivalent	7.9	5.53
Responds to name, no-no	9	6.3
Looks at pictures in book	10	7.0
Jabbers expressively	12	8.4
Imitates words	12.5	8.75
Has speaking vocabulary of three words (other than ma-ma and da-da)	14	9.8
Has vocabulary of 4-6 words including names	15	10.5
Points to one named body part	17	11.9
Names one object (What is this?)	17.8	12.46
Follows direction to put object in chair	17.8	12.46
Has vocabulary of 10 words	18	12.6
Has vocabulary of 20 words	21	14.7
Combines two or three words spontaneously	21	14.7
Jargon is discarded, 3 word sentences	24	16.8
Uses I, me, you	24	16.8
Names three or more objects on a picture	24	16.8
Is able to identify 5 or more objects	24	16.8
Gives full name	30	21.0
Names 5 objects on a picture	30	21.0
Identifies 7 objects	30	21.0
Is able to tell what various objects are used for	30	21.0
Counts (enumerates) objects to three	36	25.2
Identifies the sexes	36	25.2

Parents may elect to keep a journal recording the history of their child's physical, mental, and emotional development. The more accurate and specific the record, the more useful it will be. For example, instead of noting "Bobby learned to walk at one year of age," a more specific record would be, "At ten months, one week of age, Bobby began to take a few steps at a time without support. He would take a few steps, stop, and start again, then drop down and crawl the rest of the way."

The following guide suggests the kinds of information useful to include in such a journal.

I. Physical conditions and history
    A. Prenatal period and birth
        1. Mother's health during pregnancy
        2. Condition of birth
        3. Normal or premature birth
    B. Early developmental signs
        1. Age of holding head erect
        2. Age of teething
        3. Crawling
        4. Pulling up to standing position
        5. Age of walking
        6. Self-help skills—feeding, dressing, and the like
    C. Physical characteristics and health
        1. Height and weight chart for continued growth
        2. Right or left handed
        3. Physical impairments, if any
        4. Record of childhood diseases
        5. Injuries
II. Language development
    A. Age of talking
        1. Number of words
        2. Putting words together to make sentences
        3. Length of sentences and comprehension
    B. Age of learning to read
        1. Able to recognize words
        2. Reads sentences left to right
III. Other skills
    A. Reading interests
    B. Hobbies
    C. Other
IV. Conditions related to emotional development
    A. Signs of nervousness
        1. Sleepwalking, tummy aches, nail-biting, bedwetting
        2. Fearfulness, shyness, nightmares
    B. Social development
        1. Tantrums—at what age and frequency?
        2. Who are his or her playmates?
        3. How do they play?
        4. What does he or she do for recreation?
V. Educational experiences
    A. Age when entering school
    B. Level of cognitive functioning

     C.   Test scores of achievement or aptitude
     D.   Reports from teachers
     E.   Parent-teacher conferences
VI. A summary statement of the child in general
     A.   Strengths
     B.   Underdeveloped areas
     C.   Problems
     D.   Sources of assistance in your area

Some characteristics to look for, if you suspect your child is gifted, may be found in the various lists that have been compiled. One, developed by Dorothy Sisk (1977) shows the kind of specific detail worth recording. It includes, along with some examples drawn from older children by way of illustration, the following:

Early use of advanced vocabulary. Most children at age two make sentences like: "There's a doggie." A two-year-old who is gifted might say, "There's a brown doggie in the backyard and he's sniffing our flower."

Keen observation and curiosity. A gifted child might pursue lines of questioning such as, "What makes Scotch tape sticky on one side and smooth on the other? How can they make a machine that puts on the sticky part without getting the machine all gummed up? Why doesn't the sticky side stay stuck to the other side when you unroll the tape?"

A gifted child will also observe details. At a very young age the child might remember where all the toys go on the shelf and replace everything correctly.

Retention of a variety of information. Gifted children amaze parents and teachers by recalling details of past experiences. For example, one six-year-old returned from a trip to the space museum and reproduced an accurate drawing of a space rocket he had seen.

Periods of intense concentration. A one-year-old gifted child might sit for five minutes or more listening attentively to a story being read to an older brother or sister. Older gifted children can become engrossed in a book or project, totally oblivious to the events happening around them.

Ability to understand complex concepts, perceive relationships, and think abstractly. Although an average four-year-old looks through a picture book of baby and mother animals with interest, a gifted four-year-old is more likely to observe concepts such as how much animal mothers and babies look alike except that the baby is smaller.

If a fifth-grade class were told to write a paper on what it's like to be poor, most of the children would write, "I would be hungry" or "I wouldn't have enough money." A gifted fifth-grader would tend to view the problem more abstractly and might write something like, "Being poor would only be a problem if others were not poor. If everyone else also had very little money, then we would all have less to spend and things would be cheaper."

A broad and changing spectrum of interests. Gifted children often show an intense interest in a subject, perhaps dinosaurs, one month, then turn to a totally different subject such as French literature or railroad engines the next.

Strong critical thinking skills and self-criticism. Gifted children evaluate themselves and others. They notice discrepancies between what people say and what they do. But they are usually most critical of themselves. For example, a gifted child who has just won a swimming race might complain, "I should have beat my time by at least one second."

Parental descriptions of their gifted child's early behavior also supply the kinds of detail useful in determining a child's giftedness. For example, a dozen parents interviewed by Frinier (1978) were asked, "now that your child has been identified as gifted, can you look back at his or her early childhood and tell about something you think might have been an indication of exceptional ability?" Their responses, stimulated by items drawn from a list of gifted children's characteristics, included:

• Has displayed unusual talent in music, drawing, rhythms, or other art forms.

At three he sang songs in tune and clapped to the beat of the music on his own.

As a baby, he liked to hear recordings and have lullabies sung to him. . . He would hum many songs back in perfect tune by age one. . . at four we learned he had perfect pitch.

At three, she drew a picture of her baby sister in a buggy from side perspective. . . at five, drew a picture of tigers camouflaged in a jungle scene.

• Asks many "intelligent questions" about topics in which young children do not ordinarily have an interest.

At three while on a jet ride and the pilot came back to talk to passengers, J. became very worried and asked, "Who's flying the plane?" He often asked how things worked, such as the vaporizer, vacuum, etc. and how planes stayed in the sky.

• Keen observation and retention of information about things he or she has observed.

When H was two or three she would notice if the smallest item in a room had been moved.

His photographic memory showed up the Christmas he was three and a half. He asked us who had sent each of the seventy-five to one hundred Christmas cards and would tell the exact signature after seeing the picture on the card.

At two and a half when being instructed why streets were dangerous, he recalled the parade he had watched six months previously and said those people shouldn't have been walking in the street. At three, he would recall incidents of eighteen months previously that had not been mentioned since, such as "Remember when I fell out of the wagon and got scratched right here?" or "Remember at Christmas, not this time, but the other time, when I. . . ."

- The ability to attend or concentrate for a longer period of time than other children his or her age.

At two and a half she would play in her room for up to an hour working on projects of her own.

At three and a half he would come and tell me which Lincoln log building he was going to make and then spent up to an hour revising it.

- An early interest in clocks and calendars, and an ability to understand their function.

At three and a half he would tell me which numbers the hands were pointing to and what time he thought it was and what we should be doing (especially at seven in the morning). At four he told me he liked a digital clock better because it was easier to tell time.

- The early accurate use of a large vocabulary.

D. always used the correct word for things from the time he started talking, even four syllable words.

- Spoke in entire sentences at an unusually early age.

At age one, S. greeted all the guests at her birthday party and asked them in. Although three other children who were born on the same day attended, none of them talked in sentences as S. did.

At two he was averaging seven and eight word sentences with correct use of all parts of speech.

- The ability to tell or reproduce stories and events with great detail at an early age.

At two and a half he would tell the story of the Three Bears and imitate the voices of the bears.

• Carries on intelligent conversations with older children and adults.

He was quite tall for his age and at three and a half his playmates ranged from three and a half (whom he considered a baby) to six years of age. The five- and six-year-old boys assumed he was in kindergarten.

At four, E. described to me how a plane shudders if it is in too steep a dive.

At three he explained to me why there must be traffic lights at intersections.

• Learned to read early, with little or no formal teaching.

We didn't realize that M. was reading at age two and a half. We thought he had memorized the stories. But at age three, he picked up my golf score card and began reading the rules on the back to us.

I realized that D. was reading at age four and a half, and when I mentioned this to her kindergarten teacher, she brushed it aside. . . . Four months later, she had discovered that D. was reading at second-grade level.

• Can write short stories, poems, or letters.

He would dictate letters to me at age three.

Other information gatthered from parents, in addition to the checklist items, were:

She had a sense of humor at two and was not fooled when teased. She would turn the situation around to benefit her.

He understood cause-effect relationships at three and would theorize about what would happen.

She was extremely sensitive to the feelings and needs of others at three, had a fear of death at four.

At two she realized situations that were potentially dangerous and would tell others to be careful.

She kept eye contact with me from the minute she was brought to me in the hospital and always looked at who was holding her and talking to her.

He looked straight at the doctor in the delivery room. The doctor even commented on it.

Many parents reported that when their children were in the primary grades, they were bored, becoming behavior problems, or becoming quiet and unhappy in regular classroom settings. A definite personality change was noted by one mother, who said her son, now a surgeon, never returned to his outgoing, happy personality after entering school. His giftedness was not discovered until sixth grade, and he later was allowed to proceed more rapidly, completing pre-med and medical school in six years.

AT SCHOOL AGE

Parents must also help identify school-age gifted children. There is a tendency for teachers to nominate achievers—compliant, neat, behaving children who may or may not be gifted, while other areas of giftedness are overlooked. Identification is left to the parents, too, when gifted children hide their abilities at school, as many of them do, in order to appear more similar and more acceptable to their age peers.

Dorothy Sisk (1977) for example, has described characteristics of children who are gifted in other than academic areas—in the creative visual and performing arts and in physical psychomotor skills. Such creatively or physically gifted children demonstrate their talents early. A visually gifted child might draw a man riding a motorcycle, while classmates are still struggling to put nose, eyes, and mouth in the right places in drawing a face. Overall children who have special creative abilities will display many of the characteristics just cited as common to intellectually gifted children, but they also differ from intellectually gifted children in many ways. They are likely to have one or more of these characteristics: a reputation for having wild and silly ideas or ideas that are off the beaten track, a sense of playfulness and relaxation, a strong tendency to be noncomformist and to think independently, and considerable sensitivity to both emotions and problems.

Elizabeth Drews (1963) has described four types of gifted school-age youth, all of whom should be identified and guided along the avenues toward their potential.

The *high achieving and studious* are hardworking, striving A students who value parent and teacher expectations.

The *social leaders* value peer attitudes. Social interests come before other interests. They sometimes do well academically, but this depends on the peer group of which they are a part.

The *creative intellectuals* are divergent thinkers; that is, they look for a number of alternatives and creative answers to questions. More of the highly gifted are in this group, although they may receive lower school grades than the social leaders or high achievers. They conform neither to teachers' standards nor their age peers' expectations. They aren't the leaders, and they don't want to be. They often ask searching questions.

The last are the *rebels*. Rebels dislike rules and rebel against them. David Smith (1957) has suggested that students also rebel when neither the school nor the home environment is challenging them. They do not achieve well and may receive poor grades despite their high potential.

Parents, then, should recognize that although their child may not be achieving in school today and may even be failing, he or she may still be gifted. If they've kept some kind of early record of their child's development such as the parents' journal previously described or a baby book, it may be checked against the development table previously presented. If they still suspect that their child has outstanding potential, they should seek assistance in identification. Many schools will administer individual intelligence scales when parents request them, particularly if the child displays some problem behavior. If a local parent organization does not exist, contact the state education department official for the gifted and talented for the names of state persons or universities and colleges in your area where information is available.

These individuals often can recommend psychologists who understand gifted children to administer individual intelligence scales. This is important for accurate measurement of IQ,

2

WHAT PARENTS CAN DO ON THEIR OWN TO HELP

Once parents have confirmed that their child is gifted and are becoming comfortable with the concept, what can they do to enhance and foster his or her development? Naturally parents want their child to become a fully functioning person, free to think, to feel, to relate to others, to be himself or herself, and to succeed. This kind of person takes a lifetime to develop.

Not every gifted child has to grow up to be a world-beater or a molder of the destiny of mankind. To have brought up an ever-developing, self-directed person who feels good about himself or herself, who is productive and competent in his or her work and personal relationships, and who is able to enjoy a full and rich life is just as important.

Parents can provide the steering mechanism that will help gifted children achieve that rich, full, productive life. In many ways, their upbringing requires the same kind of guidance given all children. All children, for example, need reasonable limits. Yet gifted children often appear so competent that there is a tendency to allow too much and not set appropriate limits. Parents should strive for independence in their children, but with restraint. All children, again, should be taught to value others and to respect their rights, particularly a gifted child who may try to manipulate or control the family. No child should be excessively catered to for any reason, whether gifted, or exceptional in other ways, or an only child (Fine, 1977). Above all, parents should take time to relax and enjoy their children.

BEFORE SCHOOLING BEGINS

Early learning, however, is especially important for gifted children, and there are a number of ways parents can, with patient guidance, foster their children's learning and development before they enter school. Paul Witty (1971) suggests the following:

- Parents, as their children's first teachers, have a unique opportunity to teach by example, setting standards of reliability, honesty, thoughtfulness, and openness for their children to follow.

12

- It is important for parents to interact with their children on a number of levels —verbally, intellectually, socially, and emotionally—and more so today when TV competes for their children's attention. Parents can tell them stories and try to answer their questions in terms they readily understand. To help them use language expressively, time can be set aside when children are encouraged to tell stories. By guidance and example in the use of speech and in the art of discussion, parents can help their children learn how to reason and communicate effectively.
- First-hand experiences with a variety of children's books and magazines, puppets and puppet plays, musical instruments and children's concerts, crayons and art shows, and so on, can be offered early and adapted to each child's ability and needs. When they are difficult to provide, the local library may have resources to offer such experiences or to suggest where they may be found.
- Do not delay helping a child who requests help in printing and saying words. Many gifted children have learned to read before they enter school because appropriate opportunities have been provided during the early years. These are not children who have been pushed but rather encouraged to enjoy learning.

DURING SCHOOL YEARS

When their children are in school, parents can continue to foster their gifts in the following ways:

- By adapting to home use some of the activities used by teachers to stimulate higher levels of thinking (see Appendices 1 and 2).
- By playing more complicated games with their gifted children—for example, finding the similarity of various things seen while riding in a car, such as a telephone pole and a sign.
- By giving them time for free thinking and not overscheduling them.
- By letting them explore different things to do with household objects, giving them a chance to do something new with something old.
- By giving them periods of aloneness, as well as periods of inactivity to recoup their energy.
- By letting them daydream, a creative activity they need.
- By letting them be gullible and dumb once in a while, without correction. A person can't be right all the time, and such remarks as "See you aren't so smart" are not productive.
- By helping them to analyze themselves and their environment.

Though quick and eager to learn, gifted children may develop problems stemming from their giftedness along the way. They may have a side that educators never see. They can be noisy at school, quiet at home; quiet at school, noisy at home; a laggard with schoolwork, a pursuer of innovative projects at home; a producer at school, a TV watcher at home. Some of the characteristic problems explored by Dr. Azizolah Malukuti (1976), a clinical psychiatrist in Birmingham, Michigan, are worth noting:

- Gifted children are rather self-centered. They think mostly of themselves and, justifiably in some ways, think they are better than others. This usually makes those around them angry and critical. Even parents, whether gifted too or not, may look upon a gifted child as young as 30 months old with animosity.
- Gifted children often keep their way of thinking to themselves. The way gifted children think is different. Giftedness is a phenomenon of extraordinary perception, accompanied by extraordinary ability for abstract and comprehensive thinking, and usually (though not always) for expression. Gifted children not only have these extraordinary thinking abilities, they develop them earlier and at a faster rate. They start by perceiving the world in their own way and become inspired by their own ways of thinking and comprehending, but after several frustrated attempts to explain their methods, usually keep them to themselves, unless they can discuss them with other gifted or understanding people.
- The gifted child is instinctively motivated, whereas average children continually compare themselves with the standard set up by their parents, their school, and society at large, accept those standards, and want to conform to them. Gifted children do not like to conform. They know they are different, and they generally like themselves as they are, although as a measure of prudence, they keep such feelings to themselves. They may conform, if pushed, but in their own modified way.
- Gifted children are confident, but they are not particularly interested in appearances or in "showing off," as their parents may request. When asked to perform, for example, their presumed interest in and knowledge of politics, literature, or other adult concerns for their parents' friends, they usually do not cooperate. Not being particularly interested in what parents expect of them and inclined to be shy and introverted, they often embarrass their parents. They may want to be recognized, but not solely because they are different or gifted. Instead they often try to hide their abilities, especially from people who are interested in them only because they are different.
- Gifted children are usually interested in nature and art. They continually gain insights and information from nature and their own art work. More than that, they are regenerated by them.
- Gifted children may lack a sense of orderliness. They may be unpunctual, for example. Or if, say, they show an interest in collecting things, they are seldom

systematic or organized about it. Most gifted children are night-people. When the daily demands, stimulation, and distractions of other people are gone, these children start to bloom.

- Most gifted children seem not to seek the affection of others, including their families. At the peak of their creativity, they may seem to be hostile, sarcastic, or unfriendly. It is as if they do not recognize the feelings or even existence of others.
- Gifted children need to rest after a peak of creativity. Over-stimulation is not desirable, and when two or more gifted children get together, they usually exhaust each other. It has been observed that most gifted children and geniuses, after a peak of achievement, fall into depression, a stage of loneliness, sadness, anxiety, and fear of being left out. This is frequent in those with unlimited ability. It is a self put-down, and sadness and unwanted tears come even in very young children's eyes. This depression should be watched by parents and particular attention paid to nutrition. Let such children be alone by themselves for a period of time but not too long. Encourage them to turn to art work or perhaps take a nature walk to bring them out of their depression. If the depression lasts too long, parents may have to seek professional help.

HOW PARENTS CAN MOTIVATE THE GIFTED: SOME DOS AND DON'TS

Since a warm, nurturing atmosphere is essential to the development of a gifted child, much will depend on the parents' attitude. The most basic advice is to enjoy your gifted child and to remember that he or she is, first of all, a child.

From that follow the other attitudinal approaches that would be good for any child:

Encourage trial and error
Encourage novel ideas
Encourage goals set by the child
Encourage setting long-term goals
Help the child recognize his or her own strengths and weaknesses
Give constructive criticism
Recognize achievement
Encourage independence
Be enthusiastic and optimistic
Give honest evaluation
Set a good example in all of these areas.

Along with bringing a proper attitude to the nurturing of the child, a variety of readily available props can be arranged to further motivate a gifted child:

Furnish books that cover a wide range of subjects and reading levels
Provide reference materials and laboratory equipment
Arrange the child's room to appeal to natural curiosity
Make use of resource people in the community
Plan field trips and library visits
Set aside time for reading
Base enrichment activities on the child's interests and hobbies
Plan ways to apply what the child has learned
Encourage participation in outside activities.

One thing that should not be overlooked is the parents' need for counseling. For many parents, dealing with a gifted child is a new experience. Help and advice can be obtained from others who have wider knowledge and experience.

Those with experience will almost certainly advise you of pitfalls to avoid with a gifted child. Some of the things not to do include the following:

Don't force yourself into a teacher role all the time. You are also a parent, and your child will want you to play the parent role as well.
Don't force your child into the gifted role all the time. There are times he or she will simply want to be a child.
Don't encourage goals beyond your child's reach.
Don't give wholesale praise, but reserve it for the praiseworthy.
Don't force your child to be an "egghead" to others.
In your efforts to encourage self-direction, don't withhold direction and guidance.
Don't be afraid to admit your own ignorance about something, or be afraid to find someone else who can provide information beyond your scope.
Don't be afraid to make mistakes with your child.
Don't brag about your child's giftedness, but defend your interest in education for the gifted on the basis of providing appropriate education for all children.
Don't express your dissatisfaction with the schools in front of your child, lest it color his or her attitude toward school.

ARE YOU A GIFTED PARENT? A CHECKLIST

The more gifted a child, the more he or she needs gifted parents—parents gifted in helping him or her discover and develop his or her abilities.

This checklist is intended as a set of reminders of the most important principles for promoting a child's giftedness. Although there is no passing score, a large proportion of affirmative answers to these questions will indicate you are a parent helping to develop a child's gifts.

Do you answer your child's questions with patience and good humor?

Do you use her or his questions and expressions of interest as guides into further learning and explorations?

Do you help your child develop physical and social skills as carefully as you encourage mental growth?

Do you help your child learn how to get along with children of all levels of intelligence?

Do you avoid comparing the child with his or her brothers and sisters or companions?

Do you set reasonable standards of behavior for your child and then see that he or she meets them?

Do you impose firm, fair, and consistent discipline that is neither too harsh nor too permissive?

Do you show your child that he or she is loved for his or her own sake and not merely for intellectual achievements?

Do you avoid overstressing intellectual achievement?

Do you try to find something specific to praise when the child shows you his or her work? (A generalized compliment means little to any child.)

Do you help the child to select worthwhile reading materials and television programs?

Do you provide your child with hobby materials and books of her or his own?

Do you provide places where your child can study, work at hobbies, and display work?

Do you participate in some of your child's activities?

Do you let the child learn about and share in some of your hobbies and interests?

Do you take your child on trips to points of interest?

Do you enable your child to take advantage of lessons and activities offered by private groups or community organizations?

Do you teach your child how to budget time, organize work, and improve study habits?

Do you help your child to make his or her own plans and decisions?

Do you give your child increasing independence as his or her ability to handle responsibility increases?

Do you give the child household responsibilities and other tasks suitable for his or her age and abilities?

Do you avoid "pushing" your child too hard by not being too demanding about after school lessons or activities?

Do you resist the impulse to show off your child before relatives and friends?

Do you resist any temptation to exploit the child's gifts commercially?

Do you teach the child to use his or her gifts for the benefit of society rather than only for selfish purposes?

Do you encourage the child to set high educational and vocational goals?

Do you refrain from trying to pick the child's vocation but try to help him or her learn about as many occupations as possible?

Do your expressions of attitude and your behavior set the example you want your child to follow?

Do you avoid talking down to the child?

Do you try to speak as correctly as you want the child to speak?

3

USING RESOURCES BEYOND THE HOME

Parents turning to the schools for help in meeting the educational needs of their gifted children will find that, vital as preschool programs, early admittance, and accelerated programming are for the gifted, few such programs actually exist. Nor are they likely to develop unless school districts are able to hire teachers with the appropriate training and attitudes needed to work with the gifted, which, in turn, depends not only on an extensive reform of teachers' pre-service and in-service education, but on a more favorable attitude toward and heightened public interest in the gifted.

Parents of gifted children often become concerned enough about their child's education that they find it helpful to start or join an advocacy group for the gifted. There are many reasons to join such a group: others to talk to about similar problems with their gifted children, effectiveness in dealing with the schools, and help in getting state and local legislation, as well as national legislation, passed that will benefit their own and others' gifted children.

WORKING WITH AN ADVOCACY GROUP

How do you start? First, find out from the school principal or administration if a group exists locally. Also check with the state department of education to see if there is a state-wide advocacy group. A state group will keep you aware of state and national issues and many times help you start a group.

Suppose no group exists. What then? Start a group of your own. How do you find others? Write a letter to a newspaper, or advertise a public meeting—in the press, on educational TV or radio, or through the school or the PTA—to discuss education for gifted children. It doesn't hurt to suggest a meeting at social or church gatherings as long as the approach is one of concern for appropriate education not for a single child but for all gifted children. Meetings can be held in a school, a public library, a TV station, even a home. Anyone interested should be invited to attend. Educators as well as parents should belong to such a group, and it's good to have a representative from each school in your district attend if possible. What better way to communicate concerns and plan constructive strategies than to meet together?

The details of holding the first meeting and how to organize an effective advocacy group with staying power are given in another volume in this series, *Reaching Out: Advocacy for the Gifted and Talented* by the American Association for Gifted Children. Here the emphasis is on the parents' role.

Parents who join an advocacy group may at first feel inexperienced or timid about participating. But participation is needed—there are many jobs, large and small, to do—and parents will soon discover they do possess many leadership traits. All leaders have had to start somewhere, and joining a group should be seen as a learning experience. Parents will learn, for example, if they don't know it already, how to work with others in translating ideas into team action, how to delegate responsibility, and how to become well-informed on school matters.

Progress in education is made in small steps. Persistence and a commitment to hang on is needed when the going gets rough—when a district cuts back on programs for the gifted, a governor vetoes a bill, or a millage tax is defeated. But by winning one small issue at a time, an impressive record of victories can be had. To provide the information and fact finding needed to plan winning strategies, parents may find themselves attending school board meetings and serving on school committees, even ones that don't seem to concern the gifted directly, visiting other school districts, and asking school officials, teachers, principals, and administrators for information.

The information parents request may concern school policies, budgets, reading and math scores school by school (individual scores are confidential), specific school goals for the year, the ways parents may participate in decision making, or the way an advocacy group may help the district plan or launch programs for the gifted and talented. It's wise to put the requests in writing and to keep a record of the answers.

When working with school officials, beware of being labeled a "negative pushy parent." But don't hold back for fear of seeming "pushy." There are respectable ways of being a "positive pushy parent." It is school officials' responsibility to inform you. Don't accept vague answers. Be persistent. Keep asking specific and direct questions. Ask for a definition of educational jargon if it is used. (See Everyman's Guide to Educational Jargon in Appendix 3.)

Role-playing situations in which parents deal with school officials give good practice in learning to negotiate effectively. Some in a group take the role of school principals, teachers, or school board members. Others take the role of the public trying to make a case for gifted children and presenting it on a positive level. Table 2 lists the arguments schools often give to avoid programming for the gifted and ways to respond.

TABLE 2: HOW TO ARGUE EFFECTIVELY FOR GIFTED EDUCATION

School Argument	*Parents' Response*
We are the experts. We educators know best, and you do not understand all the complex issues involved.	Parents must persist they do know their children's needs and that it is the school officials' responsibility to design a school environment that meets the needs of *all* children.
That is not a real problem. Do you have any proof?	Be prepared to defend and define the problem. Document if possible. Do your homework and know what is happening nationally as well as in your state and locality.
The examples you cite are exceptions. It certainly isn't widespread.	Point out that each child in the school is important. Ask the school officials to prove there aren't more gifted children.
With that type of pupil, we really can't do that much.	Blaming the child rather than the system, which may be structured to create problems, is a common way to avoid facing real problems.
Yes, we know the problem exists, but we need time to figure out the best thing to do.	Ask specifically what is being done and ask for their plans in writing with a timetable and list of persons responsible for the plan.
It's an unimportant problem.	You believe the problem is important because it affects children directly.
We aren't doing worse than any other schools.	Just because other schools aren't doing anything different for the gifted does not excuse this district from providing for the needs of the gifted.
We have no money.	This may be true, but free and appropriate education of *all* children is the district's responsibility. Money should be sought from other sources, and present priorities reexamined.

If the above arguments are not productive, there are other options:

Appeal to political leaders or education officials at the state and national levels.

Legal action in the courts, a long, drawn out procedure.

Public demonstration to attract public attention. You can march on the school board offices or state capital.

Joining an advocacy group, then, will mean work, as much or as little as parents can afford to give. But it will be interesting. And it will be worth it for the gifted children in schools today and to come.

OBTAINING SCHOLARSHIPS

Scholarships are usually offered to help students attend college. Not many are offered to help students attend private schools before colleges. Parents seeking a scholarship to a private prep school should contact the school first to see if it has a scholarship fund. If not, perhaps a local community groups, such as Kiwanis, Jaycees, or Rotary, contacted personally, may be willing to sponsor your child. Some areas may also have special arrangements for sending secondary students to college classes during the year or over the summer. But in the main scholarships go to college students.

The best tip for finding college scholarships is to start early, plan, and keep trying. The junior year in high school is the prime time to start. Financial aid is available through:

- The Federal Basic Education Opportunity Grant. This is based on financial need and is available to part-time or full-time students at colleges and vocational schools, in state or out. To qualify you must complete one or two financial statements: the FAF (financial aid form) or the FFS (family financal statement), available in post offices, high school guidance offices, or at college campuses.
- A college or university's own financial aid office, which administers non-federal funds and the institution's own monies. If you are planning to seek a college's or university's financial aid, inquire about it when application for admission to the school is made. High school guidance offices can provide the names and phone numbers of financial aid directors at colleges and universities.
- State programs. Contact your state department of education to inquire about these.
- Special situation funds. These are provided by a variety of government agencies, assuming you fit their particular guidelines. Special situation funds are a narrower source of aid such as Vocational Rehabilitation Administration monies for the physically handicapped or Social Security Administration funds for students whose families receive Social Security benefits. Again, check with the high school guidance counselor.
- Private community funds, provided by clubs, businesses, unions, and civic organizations. Sometimes these groups have special scholarships. The Gifted Students Institute for Research and Development, 611 Ryan Plaza Drive, Suite 1139, Arlington, Texas 76011, suggests the following community sources for students seeking financial assistance:

1. Visit your minister, priest, or rabbi. Explain the reason you want the money, how your child will benefit, and why you need financial assistance. He should be of great help in providing funds or directing you to those who can.
2. Visit your banker. He also can give you leads.
3. Visit with your local Chamber of Commerce and explain your need. Many chapters have scholarship funds readily available.
4. Contact fraternal organizations and service clubs in your area. Some hometown organizations provide full scholarships for students to participate in unusual programs. Others pay partial fees.
5. Business and industry in your area may assist. Possibly your school faculty can give you direction on whom to contact.
6. An item in your hometown paper about your child's desire to attend college and your need for financial aid may result in funds.
7. Your doctor and dentist may be able to give you guidance and possibly assistance as they often are involved in many civic and educational efforts.
8. Look in your yellow pages under organizations, and then scan the index. You'll end up with many ideas.
9. Contact your senator or representative for assistance.

You will be amazed at how many people will help you if you just ask and present a positive picture.

Possibilities for funding differ from state to state, and it would be best to check within your own state or the state where the particular college or university is located. Above all, keep trying.

4

TWO UNUSUAL EXAMPLES OF PARENTAL EFFECTIVENESS

THE TWO EXAMPLES that follow—one of a family that guided the alternative education of a gifted child, the other of a parents group—are, in some ways, ideal in that they assume unusual resources that are not generally available. However, the underlying principles are applicable, and the examples are presented with the idea that they could be adapted to suit the circumstances of other parents and other groups.

SANDY'S SUMMER: AN EXPERIMENT IN ALTERNATIVE EDUCATION FOR A GIFTED CHILD*

Six weeks before the end of the school term, a sixth-grade girl called Sandy left school, with the permission of the principal. In part, the decision was made because the school did not know what to do for this gifted child. Sandy's family, with a natural bent toward using community resources as learning experiences, took over her education during the spring and summer.

Sandy's intelligence was higher than her performance in academic studies indicated. She scored over 130 on the Stanford-Binet and had a strong record on the Metropolitan Achievement Tests. Yet she showed no inclination to be a scholar. Instead, she consistently preferred to direct her energy into extracurricular activities such as music, band, helping in the office, and helping in the preschool room. These accomplishments were not analyzed for the skills they represent.

A few specialists demanded high-level performance from Sandy, but her classroom teacher had neither the training nor experience to deal effectively with a highly creative child. Instead, she interpreted Sandy's preference for her own areas of interest and her opinions as stubbornness.

---

*Condensation of an article by M. E. Connelly in *Roeper Review*, 1978, *12*(2).

Sandy asked to see the social worker with whom she had a good relationship. Several weeks later her parents met with the social worker, only to be told that Sandy was not getting enough attention at home. The parents countered by charging that the girl was not getting the proper attention in school, despite repeated meetings with the teacher and principal. Sandy came into the meeting to explain her feelings. When her mother asked her if she were happy in school, the child burst into tears and said that she hated school.

The social worker then suggested that Sandy design her own plans for school. This suggestion astounded the parents. If the school had been unable to give gifted children direction, how could a child do it? This was not the first time the parents had been told that they were at fault because of their child's failure to perform in school. When Sandy's oldest brother had been diagnosed a slow learner in the 50s, the mother had turned to outside enrichment for the boy, who gained from it and found it made school more tolerable for him. The boy, who scored above 135 on an individual test of intelligence, is currently working on his third degree. His problems were later diagnosed as severe learning disabilities, yet he had absorbed large amounts of information in the unstructured enrichment program planned by his family. He has said that this saved his life and sanity because of the horrors he endured at the hands of ignorant teachers.

The enrichment program for Sandy's brother was based on the mother's interest in museums and old houses. Since the other children could not be left at home, due to lack of funds for a baby-sitter, they were all, including Sandy, exposed to the same experiences at varying ages. When the mother found Sandy identifying period furniture at a landmark house at the age of two, she realized that she had completely underestimated the ability of young children to learn.

In addition to a Montessori program, the children were taken to museums, old houses, ships, bridges, factories, offices, battlegrounds, and libraries. No effort was made to teach much of anything in a formal way, but the pattern of presentation and exposure allowed the children to learn directly from the materials and make simple connections. In this way the children learned eagerly and unconsciously from the wide variety of information to which they were exposed. Their mother let them discover the world, each at his or her own level. As they grew older they rediscovered these experiences by remembering them or encountering them again, over and over, at new levels of understanding.

The experience was not a conscious effort to stimulate gifted children, but one family's way of channelling the children's energy and interests. Only much later did the parents become aware that the children were, in fact, far above average in intelligence.

Now that Sandy, the seventh child, found school stultifying, it was easy to decide to take her out of school, but the program was another matter. The older children were asked for their opinions. Sandy's siblings were now in their twenties, able to say what had helped them and what had not. For them, the field trips had meant the beginnings of a life time of intellectual curiosity.

"Do for her what you did for us," her older brother said, adding, "only don't take so many days off. There are only two rules I want you to follow. Don't ask her if she wants to go or if she likes it." This was advised by the least willing participant in the earlier learning plan.

He continued, "She will like it once she gets there, and she can't very well say if she likes something she does not know anything about. She will be glad for the rest of her life. I am."

The parents, seeing no other solution, decided to take Sandy out of school. The principal was advised and said that it was convenient to meet with them ten days hence, at which point he gave his approval. He never asked to see the journal the mother kept on Sandy nor showed any interest in the plans for the experiment.

Sandy's mother coordinated a large number of educational opportunities in the Detroit area, where they lived, to provide Sandy with a different kind of summer. Two goals were set: (1) improvement of basic skills commensurate with Sandy's potential and (2) the design and implementation of a full-scale enrichment program, broad enough for a life-time of exploration.

The basic skills were handled in two ways. Three times a week Sandy visited the Independent Programmed Learning Lab at nearby Oakland Community College, where she used programmed learning for math and reading, as well as embryology. In addition, she went to a special summer school session for experience in math gaming, computer operations, oral history, and thematic writing. (The summer session turned out not to be very valuable.)

The enrichment program needed a theme with which to coordinate all the major field trips and reading. A newspaper announcement of a performance of Shakespeare's *Othello* suggested the theme—Venice. *Othello* takes place in Venice, and the city provides a door to other subjects. Venice, 1500 A.D., became the theme.

Once a theme was determined, relevant resources appeared as if by magic.

- Shakespeare set at least three plays in Venice. Even though they were not all centered around the year 1500, their stories, the sets, the costumes and customs could be related to that specific year.
- Movies of the plays were available, and they led to the exploration of cinema for its literary and artistic merit. The theme was beginning to expand.
- The Detroit Institute of Art had just rehung the Italian Galleries, and there was a special show of Titian woodcuts. Titian led to Albrecht Durer and the history of printing. The poster for the show pictured a gold cap, which led to a study of the balance of power in the Mediterranean Sea area in the fifteenth and sixteenth centuries.

- Further reading about Venice in 1500 led to study of country houses designed by Palladio in that period.
- In 1581 the first bank was founded in Venice. This fact led to a study of banking and a visit to the State Capitol where Sandy testified at a public hearing before the banking committee in the House Chambers.
- While visiting the Legislature, Sandy learned how a bill is passed. She also met her representatives and toured the Capitol, comparing its functions and design with those of other states and with the Capitol in Washington.
- Since Venice is on the Mediterranean, it was logical to study Egypt and, on a visit to Chicago, to see the touring exhibit on King Tut. While there, Sandy also took a tour of the major architectural landmarks, visited the Art Institute to see the Chagall window and the Throne Miniature Rooms, discovered the Museum of Science and Industry, endured the Oriental Institute, and glanced at the Robie House. On the way home she explored the Indiana State Dunes State Park to compare the action of fresh water dunes with those of the Seashore National Park on Cape Cod, near where she used to live.
- A high point of her summer was a visit to her father's office on the occasion of an open house to celebrate the seventy-fifth anniversary of the first Cadillac car. The rare opportunity to observe a complete assembly line and in-depth displays in the engineering department was not nearly as important as sitting in her father's chair.
- Fascination for family stories led to an interest in genealogy. A recent find among some old papers suggested a trip to the Burton Historical Society, where they read an 1880 Philadelphia census on the microfilm reader. While there the children were asked to appear in a film about the library. Sandy's brother went to the theatre section to listen to a tape of the play in which he had appeared the previous year.
- Soon after Sandy had read the life of Marco Polo, who was born in Venice, a rerun of the Gary Cooper movie was shown on TV.
- Other field trips, not related to Venice, included Fort Wayne, library research, a tour of significant Township buildings, and concerts at Meadowbrook, Bob-Lo, and the Renaissance Center. There were also trips to Stratford, Ontario, to Windsor's Art Museum, to an exhibit on Detroit's salt mines, camping in upper Michigan, and continued study at the community college.

There were other kinds of fun as well. Sandy took riding lessons, did some sailing, and went swimming. She had several baby-sitting clients, and did volunteer work with adults in several major fund-raising projects. Her Girl Scout camping experience inspired her to become a master salesperson in the cookie campaign.

Sandy is looking forward to the Junior High School in the fall. She now says that she prefers regular school and realizes that it is up to her to "buckle down" so she will get her work done quickly and be able to go on to "more important" things. She knows that if she does not perform adequately, she will be taken out of school once again, either to study independently or go to a strict private school, neither of which she wants.

One hopeful sign is evidence of a new attitude on the part of the administration in her school district. Recently mandated provisions for gifted children may make it more likely that creative divergent thinkers will be treated with respect.

Sandy grew taller and wiser that summer. It is too soon to tell if her time had been well-spent, since there were no tests of affective development and the cognitive development needs incubation as well as testing. The only certain fact is that a young girl has been exposed to a way of development designed for the total person. Few parents are able to take the time this summer required, nor do most have the training or resources to carry out their plans and turn them into a cohesive program. However, most parents, either on their own or working with other parents, could make fuller use of such community resources as museums, libraries, theatres, exhibits, and special classes. Communities could establish a drop-in center, where parents and children could become aware of available resources and procure information and related reading on them. And, as is being done in some communities, alternative educational programs for gifted children whose needs the schools are not meeting could be instituted.

ANN ARBOR: A PARENT-DESIGNED PROGRAM FOR GIFTED CHILDREN*

The two-week Summer Enrichment Program, designed by the Ann Arbor Area Association for Gifted Children, served over 120 students in 1976, its sixth year of operation. The students, ranging in age from preschoolers through junior high, were drawn from eight schools in Michigan's Washtenaw County area. The children came because they wanted the challenge that traditional summer programs do not provide.

Since a realistic assessment of the children's interests revealed that many participated in Little League, summer band, Y camp, and local arts and crafts projects, the classes were scheduled (months in advance) for the last week in July and the first week in August when such activities for the most part have ended, and before the educational community leaves for vacation or returns to fall schedules.

For some youngsters, particularly those who have met with little competition or challenge in their regular school environment, the discovery that others, often smaller and younger, know more than they do is sobering. However, over the ten-hour period of a course, mutual respect seemed to prevail.

-----

*Condensation of an article by B. Lavery, a member of the parent group, printed in *Roeper Review*, January 1977, *12* (2), 6–7.

Class size was kept to a maximum of ten students whenever possible. At least five students had to be registered for a class for it to be offered.

The research concerning the selection of courses supported the conclusion drawn by Gina Ginsburg's work with the Saturday Workshop Program of the Gifted Child Society in Oakland, New Jersey: "Most youngsters . . . want science courses. The Society, therefore offers at least twice as many science courses as courses in the humanities and arts." Though the 24 courses chosen for the curriculum were balanced among music and art, social studies and science, the science offerings were quickly filled to capacity. Future programs may shift the emphasis heavily in favor of science and mathematics.

The most popular science classes included: "Experiments in Science" and "Discovery Science" for under seven-year-olds; "Astronomy," "Let's Explore Rocks and Minerals," and "Animals Without Backbones" for the middle childhood group. A class in "Butterfly and Plant Collecting" was cancelled early in the summer due to insufficient publicity.

"Musicology," "Animalramics" (ceramics), "Batik," "Film-making," "Stained Glass Art" and "Art of the Ancient World" composed the music and art scheduling. For the social studies buffs, "Creative Drama—Other People, Places, and Things," "All About Maps," "Bicentennial Workshop," "Anthropology—Southeast Asian Cultures," and "Mythology" were available. "Magic" and "Elementary Mathematics" emphasized productive thinking strategies.

For the preschool children, there were courses in "Orientation to the Library," "Creative Movement," "Batik," and "Main Street, Ann Arbor," among others.

Field trips and excursions were built into the curriculum, with parents acting as drivers and chaperones. Written permission from parents allowing their children to participate in these activities was required.

A number of the courses were repeated to accommodate differences in intellectual and physical development. For example, since successful performance of magic tricks often depends upon refinement of small motor skills, a class was designed for both 6-8 and 9-12 year-olds.

Teachers for the Summer Program were drawn from the faculty of the University of Michigan, Eastern Michigan University, Emerson School for the Academically Talented, Gibson School for the Gifted, and the Ann Arbor Public Schools. Classrooms and audio-visual aids were provided free of charge to the Association by the Ann Arbor Public Schools. Local artists and filmmakers as well as some versatile parents were also employed.

The fee charged for each course was $11.00. A registration fee of $4.00 per family was required, although a family could choose to join the Association for the coming year at $5.00 instead. Sixty families joined during the summer. Although membership is not necessary to enroll children, parents were urged to join and give support to future activities. Only members receive notices of special field trips and courses offered during the school year.

In assessing the effects of the program, which is totally designed and implemented by parents, the limitations of financing must be considered. Support for all classes and teachers' salaries comes from tuition. (Scholarships were awarded in the amount of $200.) Costs were kept low in order to open classes to as many families as possible.

Again because of limitations, the program did not offer the differentiated day, a goal of gifted education. Time did not permit tailoring the curricula to meet the specific abilities of individual children as would a longer, more open-ended program. No pre- or post-tests were given to determine students' academic gains, though that could easily be accomplished if it were a goal. Evaluation forms were sent to instructors and students, but the rate of return was poor. Without sufficient evaluative data, it was also impossible to assess the students in terms of measurable behavioral gains.

However, the program was successful in terms of both parent and child gratification, difficult as it is to measure that success. Parents were given a chance to directly influence their child's curriculum. There was much opportunity to suggest and hire "good teachers."

One gain in child growth and development, aside from content area knowledge, was the expansion of the students' power of self-selection. Parents were urged to let the children choose what they enjoyed, not what their parents thought they should be taking. As one nine-year-old boy stated, "In school you have to work so hard on all that other stuff that you never really have the time for the fun learning things. At the summer classes you get to think right away and have fun while you're doing it." Those who attended because their parents had chosen for them were quickly identified.

For the parent Association, the summer program has made it a viable force in the educational community. Gains in membership have added strength to its role as a regional lobbying group. Its cross-cultural impact in the rural, suburban, and urban areas of Washtenaw County cannot be matched by most local parent associations.

APPENDIX 1

BLOOM'S LEARNING THEORY AND ITS CLASSROOM USE*

Educators often refer to different learning theories. One of the most discussed in relationship to gifted students is Bloom's *Taxonomy of Educational Objectives* (1969), prepared with Krathwohl and others. Bloom's taxonomy or classification system deals with six levels of learning, each one higher than the next. (By contrast, Guilford's *Structure of Intellect* (1956) identifies more than 120 areas of learning.) Most schools concentrate mainly on Bloom's first three levels of learning:

1. Knowledge—recognition or memorization of information
2. Comprehension (cognition)—ability to translate or interpret the knowledge
3. Application—actual use of the knowledge by demonstration, such as solving math problems or making things.

Gifted children should receive more emphasis on the last three levels, which can be supplied by parents at home:

4. Analysis—comparing and contrasting the basic parts, objects, or ideas in order to draw generalizations or separate out the basic qualities
5. Synthesis—originating, integrating, and combining ideas into a product, plan, or proposal that is new or different.
6. Evaluation—judging, debating, and disputing books, articles, speeches, TV programs, or advertising.

The kinds of activities and questions teachers use at each of these levels may interest parents, since the principles and even some of the exercises can be adapted for informal home use. A guideline for teachers and sample questions follow.

---

*This material is extracted from an unpublished manuscript by Kay Coffey, *Organizing for gifted and talented*. New Orleans: n.d.

A BRIEF EXPLANATION OF THE TAXONOMY*

I.   Knowledge

In the Taxonomy *Knowledge* refers to the ability to recognize or recall information. It should not be confused with a philosophical definition. Teaching this phase of the taxonomy merely involves "pouring in" information.

This phase of instruction is usually accomplished in a formal setting. It can be accomplished with very large groups.

A. Activities usually done by student:

1. Responds to classroom situation—is attentive
2. Absorbs information—looks, listens, reads
3. Remembers
4. Practices effective procedures—drills, recites
5. Covers information in books
6. Recognizes information that has been covered

B. Evidence of student's success:

1. Completes class and homework assignments
2. Completes programmed learning sequences
3. Scores satisfactorily on objective tests

C. Activities usually done by teachers:

1. Directs student activities
2. Gives information—lectures, drills
3. Shows information—audio-visuals, demonstrations
4. Enlarges information
5. Makes and administers objective tests
6. Makes homework assignments

II.   Comprehension

Comprehension represents the lowest level of understanding. The student should be able to make some use of the knowledge that he has gained but he may not necessarily be able to relate it to other material or see its fullest implications.

------

*By Cornelia Tongue, Coordinator for Gifted and Talented, State Department of Public Instruction, Raleigh, NC.

This instruction is usually accomplished in a formal setting with a group no larger than a typical class.

A. Activities usually done by student:

1. Explains information rather than merely quotes it
2. Makes simple demonstrations
3. Translates information into his or her own words
4. Extends information to new situations
5. Interprets information from technical terms to familiar terms

B. Evidence of student's success:

1. Has the ability to intelligently discuss information
2. Can write simple essays
3. Scores satisfactorily on objective tests

C. Activities usually done by teachers:

1. Demonstrates material
2. Listens to students
3. Asks questions
4. Compares and contrasts students' answers
5. Examines students' ideas
6. Makes and administers objective tests and low level essay tests
7. Makes carefully selected homework assignments

III. Application

Application refers to the ability to use abstractions in particular and concrete situations. An example of this phase could be the using of an abstract mathematical formula to solve a specific math problem. In this phase instruction is usually rather informal. It is readily adaptable to laboratories, shops, the field, the stage, or to small groups within the classroom.

A. Activities usually done by student:

1. Solves novel problems
2. Constructs projects, models, apparatus, etc.
3. Demonstrates use of knowledge

B. Evidence of student's success:

1. Masters problem solving tests

    2. Constructs equipment, models, graphs, etc.
    3. Demonstrates ability to use equipment

C. Activities usually done by teachers:

    1. Shows students ways to facilitate their work
    2. Observes students' activities
    3. Criticizes students' activities
    4. Helps design students' projects
    5. Organizes field trips and contests

IV.   Analysis

    Analysis refers to the breaking down of a communication into its basic parts. This allows the relationship between ideas to be seen more clearly and allows basic arrangements to be studied. This phase of instruction is best conducted in an informal and irregular manner. Small group and independent study techniques are especially useful here. Homework assignments directed toward analysis have been especially valuable.

A. Activities usually done by student:

    1. Discusses information in depth
    2. Uncovers interrelationships among ideas
    3. Discovers deeper meanings and insinuations that were not apparent at first
    4. Sees similarities and differences between styles

B. Evidence of student's success:

    1. Makes effective outlines
    2. Writes effective precis
    3. Completes effective experimental write-ups

C. Activities usually done by teachers:

    1. Probes, guides, and observes students
    2. Acts as a resource person
    3. Plans for and conducts discussions, seminars, and group critiques

V.   Synthesis

    Synthesis is the putting together of elements or parts so as to form a whole. It is the arranging and combining of pieces to form a pattern or structure that was not clearly evident before. This phase of the Taxonomy is especially adaptable to independent study. It can be accomplished in almost any setting including the home. The library is especially useful. Much reflection is generally required—these results often come slowly. Patience is necessary.

A. Activities usually done by student:

 1. Produces unique communications
 2. Formulates new hypotheses based on analyzed information
 3. Makes discoveries and generalizations
 4. Shows relationships between ideas and philosophies
 5. Proposes new ways of doing things

B. Evidence of student's success:

 1. Activities above are effectively completed
 2. Writes quality essays and term papers
 3. Makes blue prints or sets of plans for projects

C. Activities usually done by teachers

 1. Extends students' knowledge
 2. Analyzes and evaluates students' work
 3. Prepares reading lists—including critical questions
 4. Brings in consultants
 5. Plans seminars
 6. Allows for independent study

VI. Evaluation

Evaluation involves making judgments about the value of materials, methods, or ideas for a given purpose. This represents the highest level of intellectual functioning. This process is difficult for even the brightest students. Results should not be expected to come quickly. Students should not feel rushed. This phase must be taught in a very informal manner and is handled best in small groups.

A. Activities usually done by student:

 1. Makes firm commitments
 2. Judges quality based on sound criteria
 3. Effectively supports or disputes ideas, theories, etc.

B. Evidence of student's success:

1. Oral and written critiques are logical
2. Speeches and essays are based on sound information
3. Projects are completed successfully
4. Performance is effective (athletic, musical, etc.)

C. Activities usually done by teachers:

1. Accepts students' ideas
2. Plans competitive essay assignments
3. Plans tournaments (speech, debates, etc.)
4. Helps establish criteria for evaluations

EXAMPLE QUESTIONS GEARED TO BLOOM'S TAXONOMY*

Knowledge
1. What is the formula for finding the circumference of a circle?
2. What are the three types of burns and standard treatment for each?
3. What nations cooperate in the European common market?
4. What is the Haber process for making nitrogen?

Comprehension—Translation
1. Translate a poem from German to English.
2. Explain the meaning of flag signals.
3. Change a written math problem into a formula.
4. Study a blueprint of a house and write an essay containing that information.
5. Change a letter into a telegram.
6. What is the meaning of "your rights stop where my nose begins?"

Interpretation
1. What do the four freedoms expressed by F.D.R. mean to you?
2. Why might some chemists write the formula for water as HOH instead of H_2O?
3. How might an ecological area change over a period of years from a sand dune into a hardwood forest?
4. What can you infer from the fact that the United States, one of the most powerful nations in the world, had been bogged down for several years in a war with a relatively weak government in Southeast Asia?

---

*An excellent reference for developing questions for each category of the taxonomy is *Classroom questions—What kinds?* by Norris Sanders. New York: Harper & Row, 1966.

5. How do you feel when you hear a train, a jet airplane, thunder, crickets chirping, or glass breaking?
6. What principle or generalization might be inferred from the following:
   a. Yon Cassius has a lean and hungry look. He thinks too much. Such men are dangerous.
   b. Fat men are jolly.

Extrapolation
1. What would life be like in the United States today if the Bill of Rights had not become part of our Constitution?
2. How might teachers and school administration change if we accept the following:
   a. The central purpose of American education is to help man become more rational.
   b. A person is rational to the extent to which he uses all available data in solving problems and to the extent that he considers all possible solutions.

Application
1. How are basic principles of conservation related to natural resorces, energy, and social relations?
2. What could a fully clothed person do to remain afloat in water for several hours?
3. What general principles of learning can be used in improving reading?

Analysis
2. Look at the *Mona Lisa* and tell which elements and principles of art were used by the artist.

Synthesis
1. Combine poetry, modern dance, music, and colored light into a presentation which emphasizes basic principles of American democracy.
2. Create a 3-D object which highlights Einstein's fourth dimension.

Evaluation
1. Decide whether or not the film *Hawaii* is an accurate portrayal of Hawaiian life at the time of the early missionaries.
2. Rate the behavior of each character in *Gone With the Wind* by first, the virtue check list that Benjamin Franklin published in his autobiography; second, The Ten Commandments.
3. Decide whether or not the United States should supply fish protein to persons in underdeveloped countries. What might be some repercussions from this act? List some of our current national problems in order of importance.

Test

1. What major formula of Albert Einstein paved the way to nuclear reactions?
2. What does the formula $E = MC^2$ mean?
3. Using your own words describe each symbol in the formula.
4. How might our lives be different today if man had not discovered how to create atomic bombs and nuclear reactors which produce electricity?
5. What relevance does this formula have for the construction of rocket engines and space vehicles?
6. Could the formula be restated in terms of social energy: number of people in a group, the time required for social action, and then be used to interpret race riots, political campaigns, and advertising campaigns?
7. What causal factors of revolution were present in recent race riots? What major factors that foster cooperation among people were present in the 1966 meeting of Premier Kosygin and President Johnson?
8. Recognizing the major factors which contribute both to revolutions and to cooperation, design a proposal by which people throughout the world could live in perpetual peace.
9. Make a list of what you think are the five most important values regarding our political, economic social system and then determine which of these tend to be most jeopardized by our participation in war.

APPENDIX 2

EXAMPLES OF LEARNING MATERIALS FOR HOME USE

W<small>ORKBOOKS AND LEARNING</small> materials that can be adapted for home use are published by a number of companies. Three examples of such firms are given here.

Engine-Uity, Ltd., P.O. Box 9610, Phoenix, AZ 85068, has developed materials for the gifted coded to Bloom's taxonomy. These may be more task-oriented than perhaps parents can manage with their children, but verbal discussions can be generated on the higher levels of thinking. Samples are included for suggested grades K-8 (see Figures 1-3). It may be that some activities may vary greatly from a child's present grade level. For example, the activities involving *Mutiny on the Bounty* (Figures 4-8) may be suited to a higher grade level. Parents are cautioned to use these materials only as a learning situation for both parents and children together. There are children who resent a parent becoming a teacher in the home. They prefer the parent to be in a parent role only. The parent-child relationship may be jeopardized if a teaching role is assumed by a parent and forced upon the child.

Midwest Publications Co., Inc., P.O. Box 448, Pacific Grove, CA 93950, has developed several workbooks to encourage critical thinking as well as inductive and deductive thinking. Gifted children find these activities both stimulating and challenging, and they can be done without instruction. The sample, Figure 9, is from the workbook, *Think About It*. Adults may also find they are fascinated by these thinking skills.

Although Kaleidoscope Press, Inc., P.O. Box 169, Blackwood, NJ 08012, offers duplicating masters in *A sourcebook of activities in: Language arts, social studies, mathematics, science for the academically talented*, there are many enjoyable things to do. Perhaps some arrangement can be worked out with your child's teacher or principal to share these materials in the school your child attends. Then your child and others too benefit from this sharing. As you can see by the sample, Figure 10, these are a little more difficult and require some preliminary instruction. Your child may even want to make up some "fair pairs" on their own.

One magazine, *Early Years*, published by Allen Raymond, Inc., P.O. Box 1223, 11 Hale Lane, Darien, CT 06820, targets its contents for teachers of preschool through third grade. In every issue in the green pages are ideas for each level. These ideas cover the social, motor, perception, math, communication, and other areas that parents of gifted preschoolers may wish to explore.

All the sample materials given in this book are meant to be supplemental. There are many other materials on the market that can prevent a child from being "bored." These will help students to learn how to use their time productively when they may be the first ones to finish their work in school or when they find themselves faced with a day alone.

FIGURE 1: SAMPLE MATERIAL FOR GRADES K-2

Valentine's Day

1. Who was St. Valentine? Write a short story about his life, then make a big paper doll.

2. Tell how you celebrate Valentine's Day by making a comic strip of St. Valentine. Use lots of boxes in a row and draw your ideas.

3. Name different ways of giving Valentines on Valentine's Day. Paste some of them on a poster and show them in your class.

4. Ask five friends to tell their feelings about Valentine's Day. Put these ideas on big red hearts and make a mobile to hang.

5. Make a new kind of Valentine and secretly give it to a friend. Say something on this new Valentine that will make your friend feel good.

6. Give a report to your class about Valentine's Day. Have a collection of things to show as you talk.

FIGURE 2: SAMPLE MATERIAL FOR GRADES 3-8

Ulysses S. Grant
(1867 - 1877)

1. Make a time line to show the major events in Grant's life.

2. Political cartoons become important tools during Grant's presidency. Make a project cube illustrating five cartoons about "Boss Tweed".

3. Find a definition for "spoils system". Apply it to Grant's administration, and write an article for a newspaper.

4. Compare Black Friday (the Panic of 1873) and Black Tuesday in 1929. Make an oral report showing similarities and differences.

5. The 15th Amendment to the Constitution insures the vote for former slaves. Write an essay predicting our society today if it had never been passed.

6. Evaluate Grant's eight years as a president. Make a chart. Divide it into two parts. Decide which events in his administration were positive and which were negative.

FIGURE 3: SAMPLE MATERIAL ON SPORTS FOR ASSORTED GRADES

Ice Hockey

1. Make a project cube listing the players of a professional ice hockey team and name the positions they play.

2. Teach a lesson to demonstrate a wrist shot and a slap shot.

3. Construct a model of an ice hockey rink. Make it to scale.

4. Make a diagram of the protective equipment worn by the goalie.

5. Translate the excitement of an ice hockey game by making a collage of action pictures.

6. Criticize the violence of an ice hockey game. Organize a debate to examine both sides of the issue.

FIGURE 4: SAMPLE *MUTINY ON THE BOUNTY* **MATERIAL FOR MORE ADVANCED STUDENTS**

MUTINY ON THE BOUNTY
PORTA-CENTER WORKSHEET

REQUIRED READING: Nordhoff, Charles, and Hall, James Norman. *Mutiny on the Bounty.* Boston: Little, Brown, 1951.

1. Why was Captain Bligh so greatly disliked?_____
_____
_____
_____

2. Why did Roger Byam sign on?_____
_____
_____
_____

3. Describe Tahiti in three sentences._____
_____
_____
_____
_____

4. Why did Christian mutiny?_____
_____
_____
_____

5. Why was Byam court-martialed?_____
_____
_____
_____
_____

6. What happened to Bligh?_____
_____
_____

7. Is this a true story?_____

MUTINY ON THE BOUNTY
(answer key)

1. Bligh was a brutal disciplinarian. He often had seamen flogged for minor offenses. He publicly criticized his officers and hoarded food and luxuries for himself.

2. Byam was to write a dictionary of the language of the natives of the South Sea Islands.

3. Tahiti was a tropical island paradise of warm weather, plentiful food and happy natives. Tahiti had mountains, rivers, uplands and coral beaches. The population was friendly and willing to cooperate with the *Bounty*.

4. Christian had been the object of Bligh's anger time and again. He had been embarrassed, harassed and shamed. Christian could not live through another year of it.

5. Byam was left behind when Bligh and those who supported him were cast adrift. Bligh accused Byam of participating in the mutiny.

6. Bligh and eighteen men were cast adrift in the launch. They eventually reached the Dutch Islands and returned to England.

7. Yes.

FIGURE 5: SAMPLE *MUTINY ON THE BOUNTY* MATERIAL FOR MORE ADVANCED STUDENTS

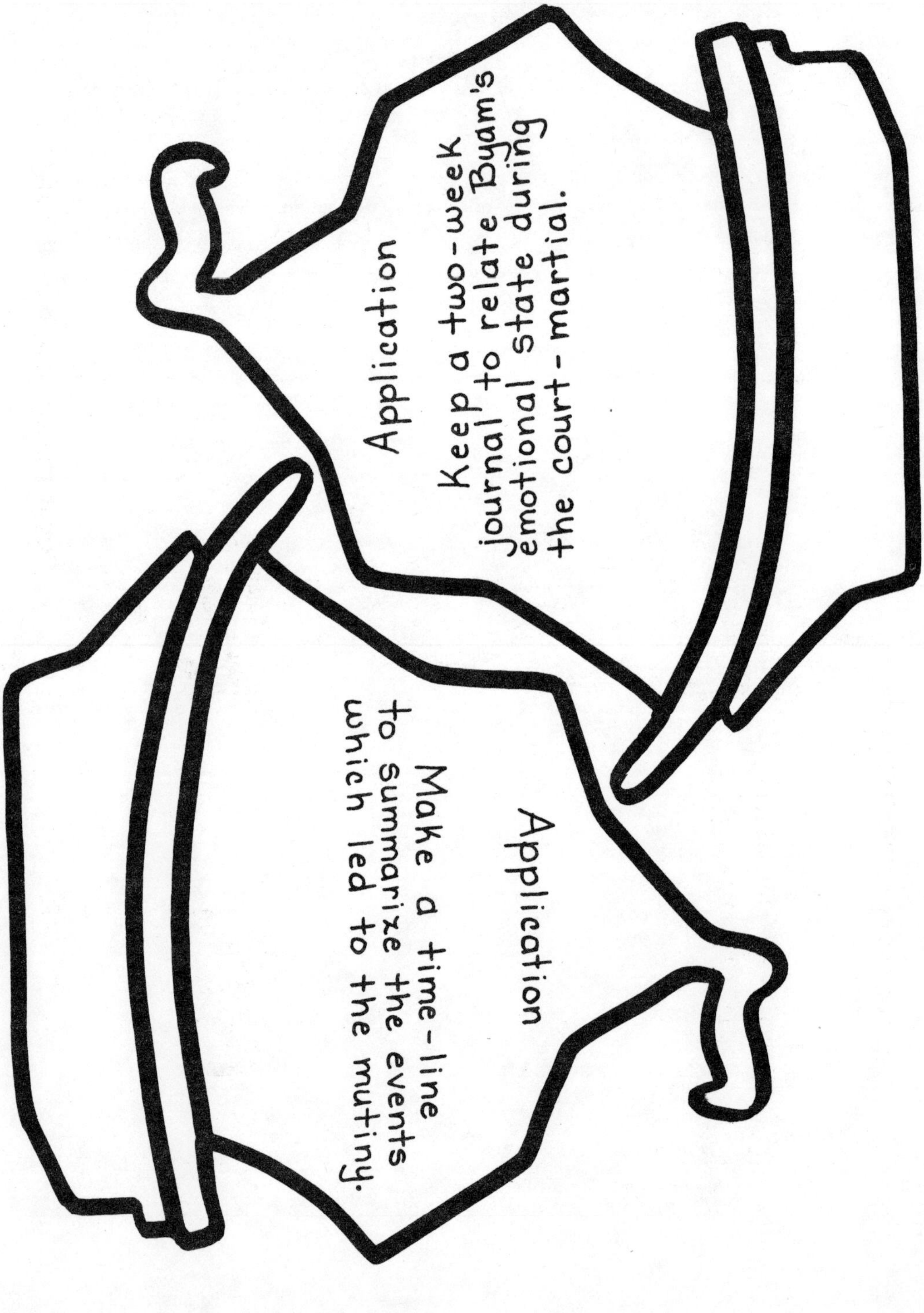

FIGURE 6: SAMPLE *MUTINY ON THE BOUNTY* MATERIAL FOR MORE ADVANCED STUDENTS

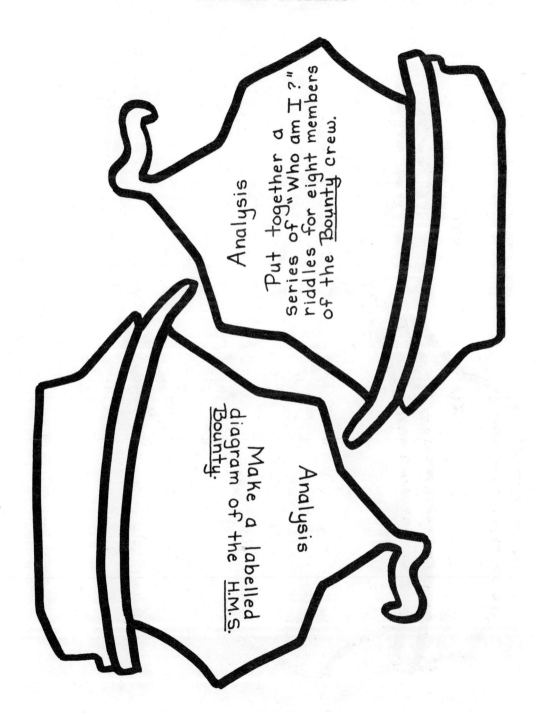

Analysis

Put together a series of "Who am I?" riddles for eight members of the Bounty crew.

Analysis

Make a labelled diagram of the H.M.S. Bounty.

**FIGURE 7: SAMPLE *MUTINY ON THE BOUNTY* MATERIAL FOR MORE
ADVANCED STUDENTS**

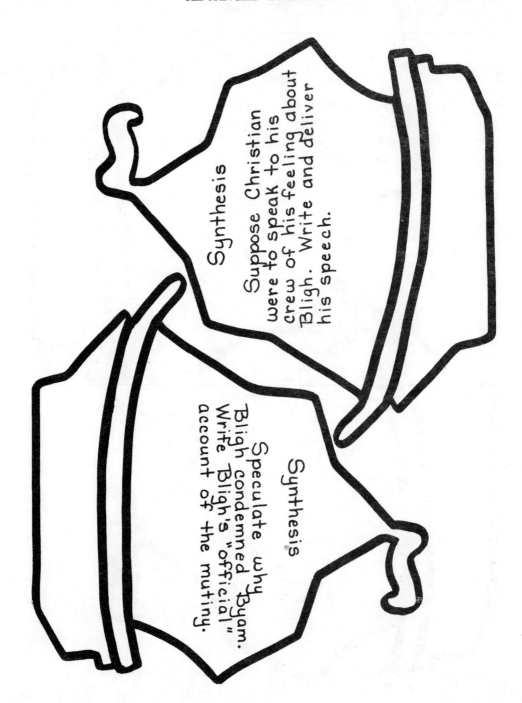

FIGURE 8: SAMPLE *MUTINY ON THE BOUNTY* MATERIAL FOR MORE ADVANCED STUDENTS

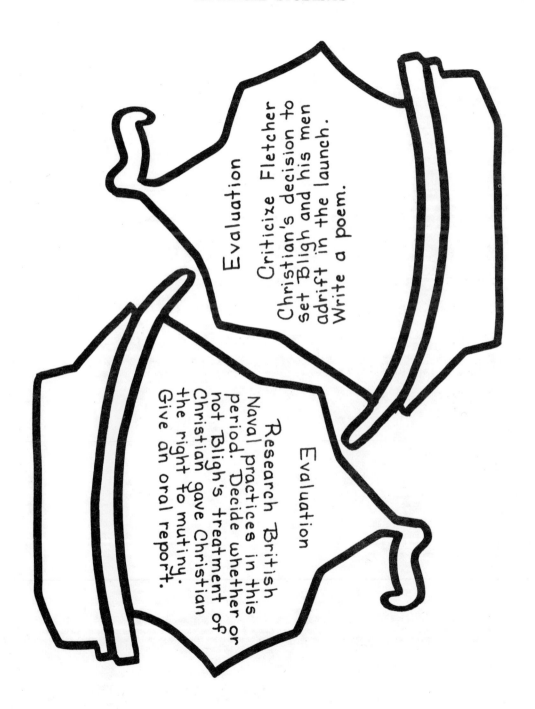

Evaluation

Criticize Fletcher Christian's decision to set Bligh and his men adrift in the launch. Write a poem.

Evaluation

Research British Naval practices in this period. Decide whether or not Bligh's treatment of Christian gave Christian the right to mutiny. Give an oral report.

FIGURE 9: SAMPLE OF BASIC THINKING SKILLS MATERIAL FROM
THINK ABOUT IT

5. Lynn, Mickey, and Tracy were the best reader, speller, and artist in the class. Lynn was taller than the best speller. Mickey was younger than the best artist. Mickey was taller than Lynn. Which student was the best reader? speller? artist?

Answer: Best reader, Mickey; best speller, Tracy; best artist, Lynn.

© 1977 Midwest Publications Co., Inc.

FIGURE 10: SAMPLE LANGUAGE ARTS MATERIAL FROM
A SOURCEBOOK OF ACTIVITIES

FAIR PAIRS

This is a rhyming activity. The definitions on the left require a rhymed pair of words—a fair pair—for an answer. For example:

A tiny sphere is a *small ball.*

See if you can do these FAIR PAIRS.

An evil grin is a <u>vile</u> *smile.*
An angry employer is a <u>*cross* boss</u>.
A fish doctor is a <u>*sturgeon* surgeon</u>.
A happy canine is a <u>jolly *collie.*</u>
An elegant Arab is a <u>*chic* sheik</u>.
These are a little bit harder. You have to supply both words!
A big flat boat is a <u>*large* barge</u>.
An addiction to stylish clothes is a <u>*fashion* passion</u>.
A Pope's tree is a <u>*papal* maple</u>.
A problematic pronunciation is a <u>*friction* diction</u>.
An angry father is a <u>*mad* dad</u>.
A kitchen knife is a <u>*butter* cutter</u>.
One rhyme is a <u>*single* ·jingle</u>.
An obese feline is a <u>*fat* cat</u>.

Now do it in reverse. The rhymed words are supplied. You give the definition.

A stout trout is a <u>*fat* fish</u>.
A plain Jane is a <u>*homely* girl</u>.
A wan swan is a <u>*pale* cygnet</u>.
A sage gauge is a <u>*wise* thermometer</u>.

Now it's your turn. See how many Fair Pairs you can make up on your own.

APPENDIX 3

EVERYMAN'S GUIDE TO EDUCATIONAL JARGON*

Thomas G. Banville

Ability Grouping: Bringing together children at the same achievement level (or with similar potential) for purposes of instruction.

Ability Test: An examination purported to measure a child's educational potential; also IQ test.

Acceleration: Advancing a child beyond the normal grade level for his or her age; also called "skipping."

Achievement: The degree to which a child assimilates learning tasks presented in the classroom.

Achievement Test: A device used to measure how much of what has been taught a child has learned.

Affective: Pertaining to the emotional aspects of human behavior; affects feelings.

Basic Skills: The kinds of learnings (recognition of colors, sizes, shapes, and positions; fine motor abilities, etc.) considered necessary to begin formal education.

Chronological Age (CA): The age of an individual expressed as years, months, and days.

Cognitive: Pertaining to ideas or thoughts.

Creativity: Searching for and finding new relationships between concepts and new solutions to problems.

Diagnostic/Prescriptive Teaching: An approach which uses an ongoing teaching-testing-teaching process. First the strengths and weaknesses of the individual are analyzed and then specific objectives are designed to correct the deficiencies.

Distractibility: The inability to attend to incoming information which is pertinent to the solution of the problem at hand; inability to keep one's mind on a task.

Early Childhood Education (ECE): Specifically, a program designed to insure the successful completion of grades kindergarten through three by identifying areas of weakness and providing special assistance.

---

*Reprinted with permission of the publisher, Allen Raymond, Inc., Darien, CT 06820, from the January 1977 issue of *Early Years*.

Ego: The self; the core of one's personality.

Emotional Block: Temporary impairment of learning ability due to stress (frustration, anxiety, pressure, etc.).

Experience Approach: A reading instruction method that uses a child's own experiences. Children tell something important to them and it is typed and read to or by them.

Fast Learner: One who is able to acquire skills or knowledge at a significantly faster rate than others.

Fine Motor: Pertaining to the use of small muscles, such as those of the fingers or eyes. (*See also* gross motor)

Gifted: Intellectual achievement which places a person at the top two percent of all those measured; an IQ of around 130. (*See also* IQ)

Grade Equivalent Score: An achievement test score which is expressed in terms of school year and month. For example, a score of 3.8 means achievement equal to that expected at the eighth month of the third grade.

Gross Motor: Refers to the large muscles, such as those controlling the arm or neck. (*See also* fine motor)

Hyperactivity: Excessive or exaggerated muscular activity; also hyperkinesis (hyper = increased, kinesis = motion).

Hypoactivity: Decreased motor activity, also hypokinesis (hypo = decreased).

IEP: Individual Education Plan.

Illinois Test of Psycholinguistic Abilities (ITPA): A test designed to measure the young child's age (2 1/2 to 9) ability to receive and express language.

Immaturity: Generally, unreadiness to undertake an educational task or tasks or to profit from a structured educational experience. Reasons may be physical, social, or psychological or some combination of these.

Individualized Instruction: An educational approach that, in each sub-area of instruction, deals with individual differences.

Intelligence Quotient (IQ): The relationship of an individual's mental age (MA) to his chronological age (CA); the mental age divided by the chronological age and multiplied by 100. (A mental age of 5 years, 10 months at the chronological age of 5 years, 10 months yields an IQ of 100.)

Isolate: A child who is excluded from (or excludes herself or himself from) the society of classmates, schoolmates, or friends; a "loner."

Language Arts: Includes reading, writing, spelling, speech, listening—all aspects of communication. Reading is generally accorded a separate designation, thus, "reading and language arts."

Learning Disability Group (LDG): A small-group instructional arrangement for children who have learning disabilities. Children spend only a part of the day in the group setting, as compared to the E.H. (educationally handicapped) group, which may be a full-day program.

Look-Say: A method of teaching reading, which relies primarily on the visual recognition of words. Often this is incorrectly referred to as the "look-see" method. (*See also* phonetic)

Mastery: Successful performance of an educational task at a predetermined level of proficiency.

Mean: The mathematical average, or the total of the scores divided by the number of scores.

Median: The middle score in a group of scores arranged from high to low or vice-versa.

Mental Age (MA): A measure of mental attainment obtained by testing. An individual who does as well as the average 10-year-old does on such a test has an MA of 10 years.

Multi-Age Grouping: An instructional organization in which children of several different ages are in a single classroom with each child proceeding at his or her own pace.

Objective Measurement: An evaluation (or scoring) which is supposedly independent of any bias on the part of the person doing the evaluating.

Open Classroom: In general, a classroom so arranged that the individual child is encouraged to follow her or his own interests. The teacher is a manager and a facilitator of learning.

Peer Group: One's intellectual and/or social and/or educational equals.

Percentile: A score which ranks an individual relative to those who fall below or above him or her. For example, a score at the 58th percentile means that out of every 100 persons tested, 58 would fall below and 42 above.

Performance Objective: An educational task which is described in terms of who will do it, under what conditions, at what time, the standard acceptable, and how attainment will be measured. For instance, a reading objective for children may be that they will learn all the beginning consonants after three weeks of instruction as measured by a test the teacher has devised.

Phobia: An unreasoned fear which produces great anxiety. Usually the victims of a phobia will indulge in an activity which permits them to escape what they believe to be the object of their fear. (*See also* school anxiety)

Phonics or Phonetic: In general, a reading approach that primarily focuses on the sounds of words as they relate to their written representations. (*See also* look-say)

Plateau: A period of no apparent progress in learning. (A new approach may be necessary, or the child may merely be "getting it all together" before going on to the next step.)

Prognosis: An educated guess—one based on available information—as to the future course of a condition or situation.

Projective Test: A series of open-ended questions or similar techniques that induce individuals to provide information about their personalities by projecting themselves into a response. (One well-known projective test uses ink blots and asks the individual being tested to tell the examiner what each ink blot looks like to her or him.)

Psycholinguistics: The study of the mental processes underlying the acquisition and use of language.

Psychometrist: One who is trained to administer psychological tests.

Psychomotor: Activity involving both physical and psychological aspects.

Rapport: A relationship characterized by mutual confidence and cooperation.

Reading Readiness: The stage of development at which, under ordinary circumstances, a child is ready to begin reading. Neurological, physiological, social, emotional, and other factors must be considered.

Reality Therapy: A psychiatrist approach developed by Dr. William Glasser, which, as applied to the classroom, stresses increased involvement of the child in the educational process.

Regression: A retreat to a lower stage of maturity. Regression sometimes occurs when stress threatens the integrity of the ego. (*See also* ego)

Reinforcement: Experiences and activities designed to support something already taught. Also a term used in the behavior modification approach that is known as "operant conditioning." In this case, reinforcement means immediately following a desired behavior with something (very loosely, a reward) which is likely to cause a repetition of that behavior.

Reversal: The tendency to read or write backward (was for saw, for example, or b for d).

School Phobia: An anxiety which is manifested in a fear of school and a refusal to attend.

School Psychologist: A specialist trained in the administration of objective and projective tests. She or he can measure ability, analyze personality patterns and provide diagnostic and prescriptive information. In some cases, they also provide therapy.

Self-concept: One's overall opinion of himself or herself.

Sibling: A brother or sister.

Standardized Test: A test that has been given to enough individuals to provide a scale of performance expectations (e.g., a standard established for a particular age or a particular grade level).

Stanine (standard nine): A score which indicates placement on a nine-point scale. A score of 5 is the median. (*See also* median)

Stimulus: Anything in an individual's environment that can arouse a reaction or response.

Subjective Measurement: A measurement which involves, at least to some extent, the impressions, intuitions, or hunches of the person doing the measuring.

Underachievement: Educational attainment below one's evidenced ability.

Values Clarification: An educational adjunct which exposes children to an examination of their own ideals so that they learn to make choices based on their own value systems.

Withdrawal: Behavior characterized by shyness, over-conformity, feelings of inadequacy and unimportance, fear, and anxiety. Often withdrawn children are ignored because they are not seen as behavior problems. Untreated, withdrawal can become very serious and may lead to childhood schizophrenia.

REFERENCES

Bloom, B. *Taxonomy of educational objectives*. New York: McKay, 1969.

Coffey, K. *Organizing for the gifted and talented*. Unpublished manuscript, n.d. (Available from 1627 Frankfort St., New Orleans, LA 70122.)

Connelly, M. Sandy's summer. *Roeper Review* (formerly *Parent Communication*, Roeper City and County School, Bloomfield Hills, MI), 1978, *12*(2).

Drews, E. Four faces of able adolescents. *Saturday Review*, 1963, *46*(3), 69–71.

Ellis, J. *Somewhere to turn*. Unpublished manuscript, University of Michigan, 1977.

Fine, M. Facilitating parent-child relationships for creativity. *Gifted Child Quarterly*, 1977, *21* (4), 487–500.

Frinier, J. *The young gifted child: Identification, programs, and problems*. Unpublished manuscript, University of Michigan, 1978.

Guilford, J. Structure of intellect. *Psychological Bulletin*, 1956, *53*, 267–293.

Harnadek, A. *Think about it: Basic thinking skills*. Troy, MI: Midwest Publications, 1977.

Lavery, B. Ann Arbor summer programs. *Roeper Review* (formerly *Parent* Communication, Roeper City and County School, Bloomfield Hills, MI), *11*(2), 6–7.

Malakuti, A. *The mental health of gifted children*. Unpublished manuscript, 1976. (Available from 4116 West Maple Road, Birmingham, MI)

Oliver, A. I., Glatthorn, A., & Smith A. R. *A sourcebook of activities in language arts, social studies, mathematics, science for the academically talented* (4 vols., Gr. 4–6). Blackwood, NJ: Kaleidoscope Press, 1978.

Sisk, D. *Teaching gifted children* (publication developed in conjunction with a federal project from Title V, Sec. 505), n.d.

Sisk, D. What if your child is gifted? *American Education*, 1977, *13*(8), 23–26.

Smith, D. *Gifted children in tomorrow's world*. Tucson: College of Education, University of Arizona, 1957.

Thinking CAPS. *Materials for gifted—cognitive, affective, psychomotor, skills and activities*. Phoenix (Box 7239): n.d.

Witty, P.A. *Reading for the gifted and creative student*. Newark, DE: International Reading Assn., 1976.

BIBLIOGRAPHY

Burroughs, M.C. *Restraints on excellence: Our waste of gifted children*. Lewiston, ID: Orchards Publishing, 1977.

California State Department of Education. *Principles, objectives, and curricula for programs in the education of mentally gifted minors, kindergarten through grade twelve*. Sacramento: 1971.

Davies, D. *Schools where parents make a difference*. Troy, MI: Midwest Publications, 1976.

National Committee for Citizens in Education. *Developing leadership for parent/citizen groups*. Columbia, MD: 1976.

Smith, C.E. *Better meetings: A handbook for trainers of policy councils and other decision-making groups*. Atlanta, GA: Humanics Press, 1975.

RESOURCES

Contact your State Department of Education for present address of a state group or local group.

American Association for Gifted Children
15 Gramercy Park
New York, NY 10003

ERIC Clearinghouse on Handicapped and
    Gifted Children
1920 Association Drive
Reston, VA 22091

Gifted Students Institute
611 Ryan Plaza Dr., Suite 1139
Arlington, TX 76011

National Association for Gifted Children
217 Gregory Drive
Hot Springs, AR 71901

National/State Leadership Training In-
    stitute on the Gifted and Talented
316 W. Second St., Suite PH-C
Los Angeles, CA 90012

Office of Gifted and Talented
United States Office of Education
Room 2100, ROB 3
7th and D Streets, S.W.
Washington, D.C. 20202

The Association for Gifted
Council for Exceptional Children
1920 Association Drive
Reston, VA 22091

World Council for Gifted Children
(Contact Office of Gifted and Talented for
    present address)

INDEX

Montessori program, 25
Motor ability, 2–3, 29
Museums, 25, 27–8
Music, 7, 13, 24, 29

National Association for Gifted Children,
   58
National/State Leadership Training Institute on the Gifted and Talented, 58
Natural science, 14–5

Oakland Community College (MI), 26

Parent-Teachers Association, 19
Parents: helping gifted children, 12–18;
   identifying gifted children, 1–11; in ad-
   vocacy groups, 19–22; in summer pro-
   grams for the gifted, 24–30
Peers, 10
Performing arts, 10
Prep schools, 22, 28
Programmed learning, 26
Psychomotor skills, 10
Puppets, 13

Questions (children's), 17

Reading, 5, 9, 20; books and magazines, 13,
   16–7, 26
Rebels, 10
Role-playing in advocacy, 20–1

Scholarships, 22–3, 30

Science, 29, *See also* Natural science
Sensitivity, 10
Shakespeare, William, 26
Shyness, 14
Siblings, 1, 17, 25–6
Sisk, Dorothy, 6, 10
Slosson Intelligence Test, 2
Social Security Administration, 22
Social studies, 29
Social workers, 25
Stanford-Binet intelligence quotient (IQ), 25
Story-telling, 8, 13
Study habits, 17
Summer programs for the gifted, 24–30;
   funding for, 29–30

Teachers, 19, 25
Television, 13–4, 17, 19
Tests, 6, 11

United States Office of Education, Office of
   the Gifted and Talented, 58
University of Michigan, 29

Visual arts, 10
Vocabulary, 4, 6, 8
Vocational Rehabilitation Administration,
   22

Washtenaw County (MI), 28–30
World Council for Gifted Children, 58
Writing, 9, 26